ONE DIRECTION

T0060787

ISBN 978-1-4950-0198-7

HAL•LEONARD®
CORPORATION
7777 W. BLUEMOUND RD. P.O. BOX 13819 MILWAUKEE, WI 53213

Visit Hal Leonard Online at
www.halleonard.com

STRUM AND PICK PATTERNS

This chart contains the suggested strum and pick patterns that are referred to by number at the beginning
of each song in this book. The symbols ⊓ and ∨ in the strum patterns refer to down and up strokes, respectively.
The letters in the pick patterns indicate which right-hand fingers play which strings.

p = thumb
i = index finger
m = middle finger
a = ring finger

For example; Pick Pattern 2
is played: thumb - index - middle - ring

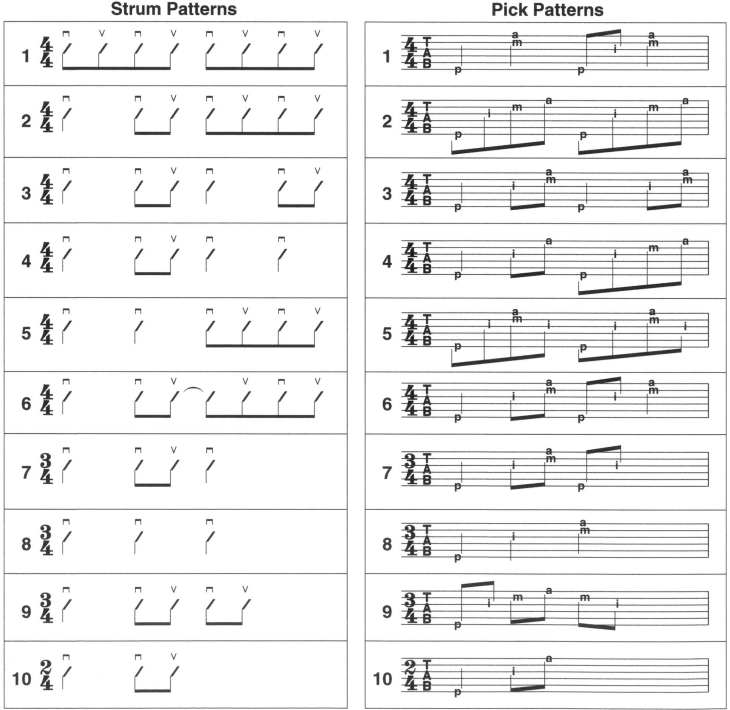

Strum Patterns   **Pick Patterns**

You can use the 3/4 Strum and Pick Patterns in songs written in compound meter (6/8, 9/8, 12/8, etc.).
For example, you can accompany a song in 6/8 by playing the 3/4 pattern twice in each measure.
The 4/4 Strum and Pick Patterns can be used for songs written in cut time (₵) by doubling the note
time values in the patterns. Each pattern would therefore last two measures in cut time.

Happily

Words and Music by Carl Falk, Savan Kotecha and Harry Styles

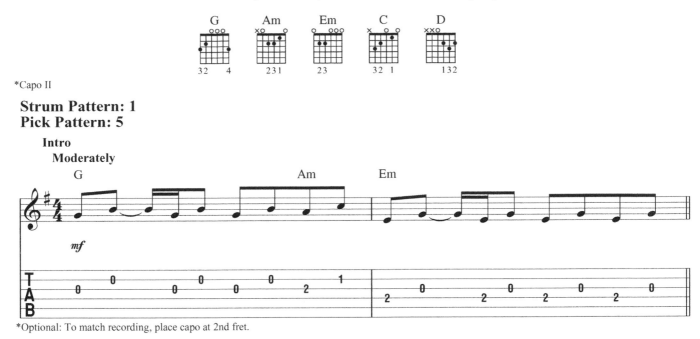

*Capo II

Strum Pattern: 1
Pick Pattern: 5

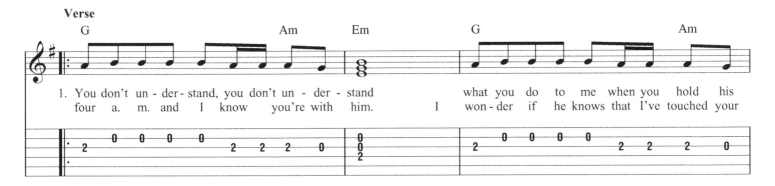

*Optional: To match recording, place capo at 2nd fret.

1. You don't un-der-stand, you don't un-der-stand what you do to me when you hold his
   four a. m. and I know you're with him. I won-der if he knows that I've touched your

hand. We were meant to be, but a twist of fate
skin. And if he feels my trac-es in your hair, I'm

made it so we had to walk a-way.) 'Cause we're on fi-re, we __
sor-ry, love, but I don't real-ly care.)

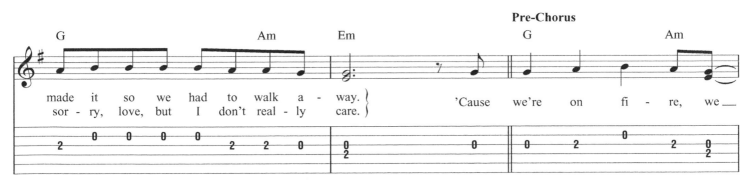

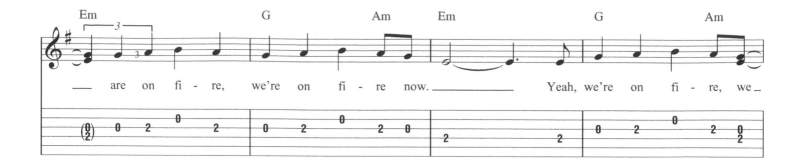

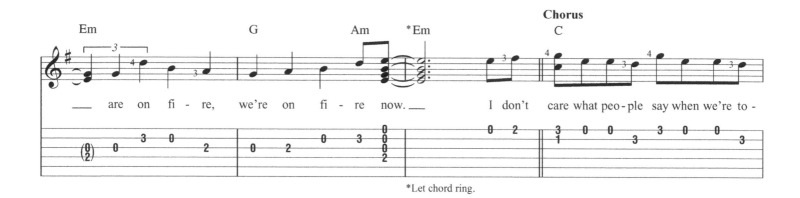

*Let chord ring.

**First time, let chord ring.

*Let chord ring.

5

Best Song Ever

Words and Music by Edward Drewett, Wayne Hector, Julian Bunetta and John Ryan

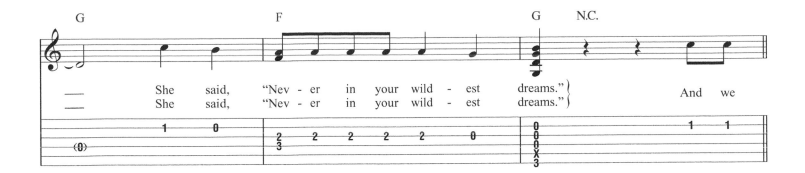

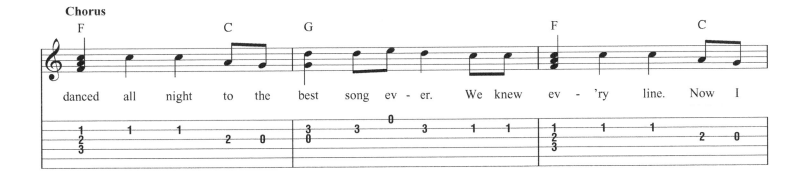

She said, "Nev-er in your wild - est dreams."
She said, "Nev-er in your wild - est dreams." And we

Chorus

danced all night to the best song ev - er. We knew ev - 'ry line. Now I

can't re - mem - ber how it goes, but I know that I won't for - get her. 'Cause we

danced all night to the best song ev - er. I think it went, oh, oh, oh. ___ I think it went,

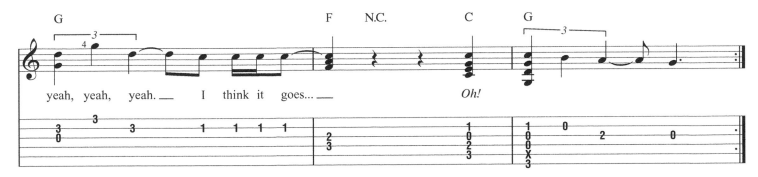

yeah, yeah, yeah. ___ I think it goes... ___ *Oh!*

7

Bridge

You know I know you know ___ I'll re-mem-ber you. And I know you know I know __

__ you'll re-mem-ber me. And you know I know you know ___ I'll re-mem-ber you. And

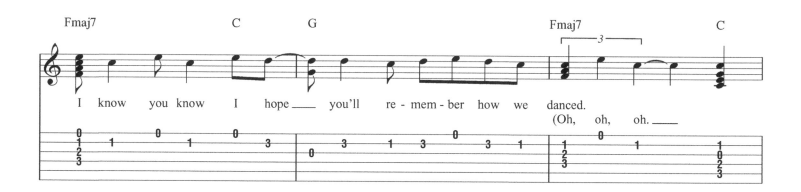

I know you know I hope ___ you'll re-mem-ber how we danced.
(Oh, oh, oh. ___

w/ Lead. Voc. ad lib.

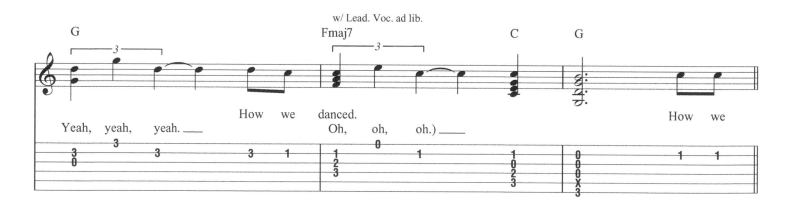

Yeah, yeah, yeah. ___ How we danced. How we
Oh, oh, oh.) ___

Chorus

danced all night to the best song ev-er. We knew ev-'ry line. Now I

can't re-mem-ber how it goes, but I know that I won't for-get her. 'Cause we

danced all night to the best song ev-er. And we best song ev-er. I think it went,

oh, oh, oh.___ I think it went, yeah, yeah, yeah.___ I think it goes...___

Outro

___ Oh! Best song ev-er.

Repeat and fade

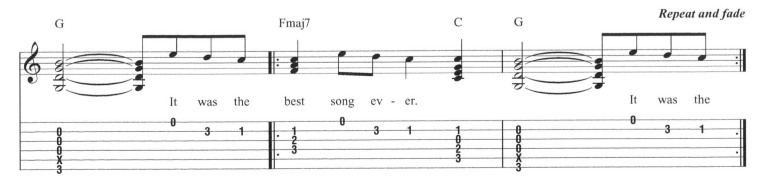

It was the best song ev-er. It was the

Diana

Words and Music by John Ryan, Jamie Scott, Julian Bunetta, Liam Payne and Louis Tomlinson

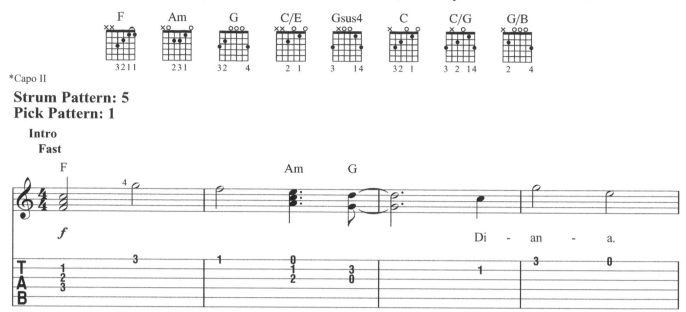

*Capo II

Strum Pattern: 5
Pick Pattern: 1

Intro
Fast

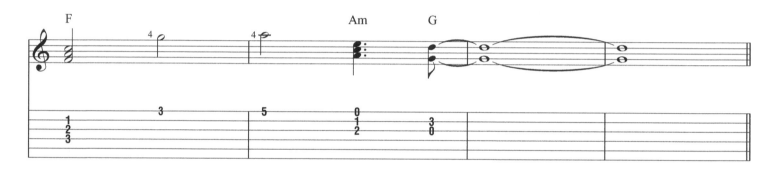

Di - an - a.

*Optional: To match recording, place capo at 2nd fret.

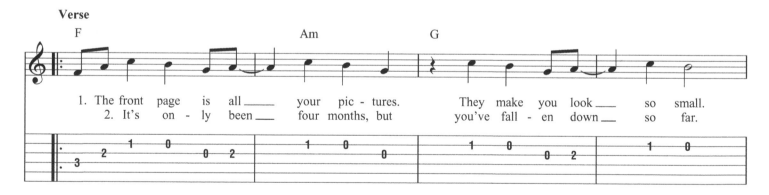

1. The front page is all _____ your pic - tures. They make you look ___ so small.
2. It's on - ly been ___ four months, but you've fall - en down ___ so far.

Verse

How could some - one _____ not miss ___ you at all? (Oh.) _____
How could some - one _____ mis - lead ___ you at all? (Oh.) _____

I nev - er would __ mis - treat you. No, I'm not a crim - i - nal.
I wan - na reach __ out for you; I wan - na break __ these walls.

I speak a dif - f'rent lan - guage, but I still hear { your / you } call. Di -

𝄋 Chorus

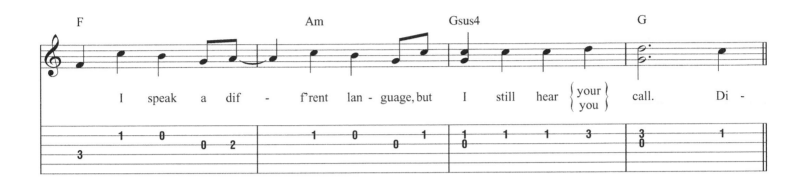

an - a, let me be the one to light a fire in - side those eyes.

*3rd time, let chords ring (next 4 meas.)

You've been lone - ly, you don't e - ven know me, but I can feel you

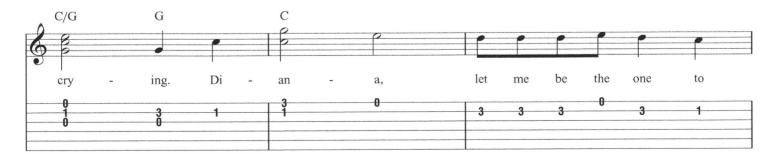

cry - ing. Di - an - a, let me be the one to

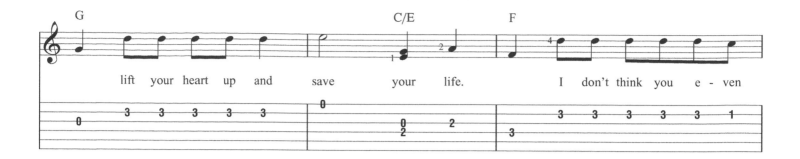

lift your heart up and save your life. I don't think you e - ven

3rd time, To Coda ⊕

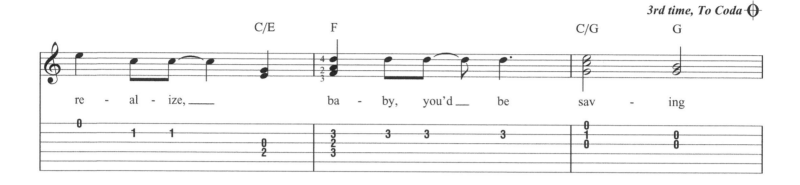

re - al - ize, _____ ba - by, you'd _ be sav - ing

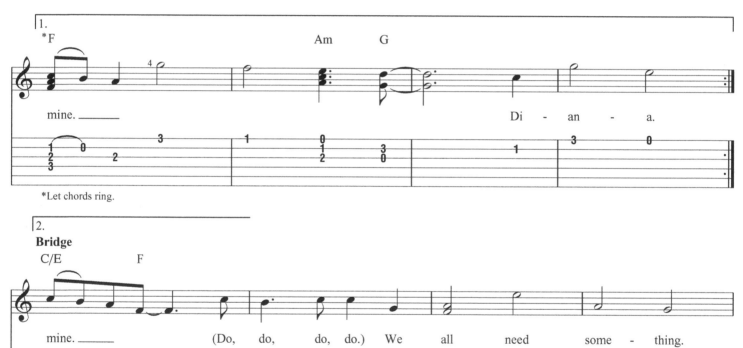

1.

mine. _____ Di - an - a.

*Let chords ring.

2.

Bridge

mine. _____ (Do, do, do, do.) We all need some - thing.

(Oo. _____ Do, do, do, do.) This can't be o - ver

now.   (Do,   do,   do,   do.) If   I   could   hold   you,

D.S. al Coda

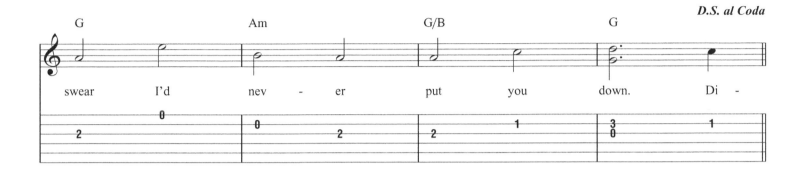

swear   I'd   nev –   er   put   you   down.   Di –

⊕ Coda
Outro

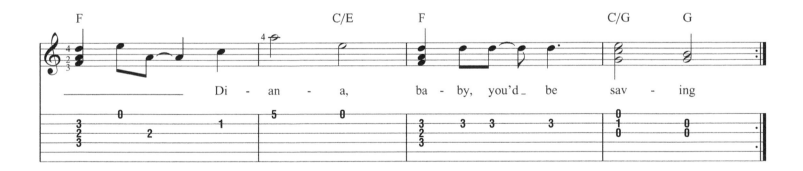

mine.   (Oh.) _____ Di – an –   a.   (Oh.) _____

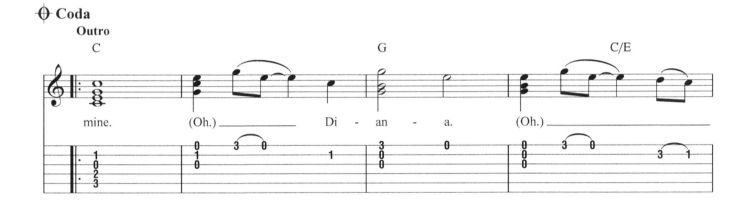

_____ Di – an –   a,   ba – by, you'd be   sav – ing

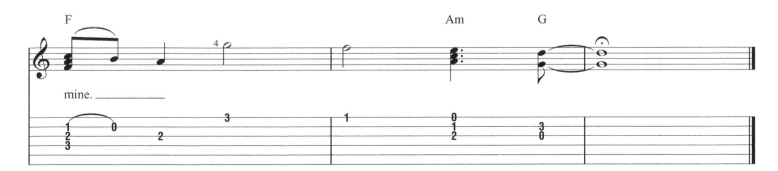

mine. _____

Kiss You

Words and Music by Shellback, Savan Kotecha, Kristian Lundin, Rami Yacoub, Carl Falk, Kristoffer Fogelmark and Albin Nedler

*Capo IV

Strum Pattern: 4
Pick Pattern: 1

Intro
Fast

*Optional: To match recording, place capo at 4th fret.

1. Oh, I just wan-na take you an-y-where that you like. __ We could go out an-y day, an-y night. __ Ba-by, I'll take you there, __ take you there. Ba-by, I'll take you there, __ yeah. Oh, tell me, tell me, tell me how to turn your love

2. Oh, ba-by, ba-by, don't you know, you got what I need, __ look-ing so good from your head to your feet. __ Come on, come o-ver here, __ o-ver here. Come on, come o-ver here, __ yeah. Oh, I just wan-na show you off to all of my

on. _____ You can get, get an-y-thing that you want. _ Ba - by, just
friends, _ mak-ing them drool down their chin-ny-chin - chins. _ Ba - by, be

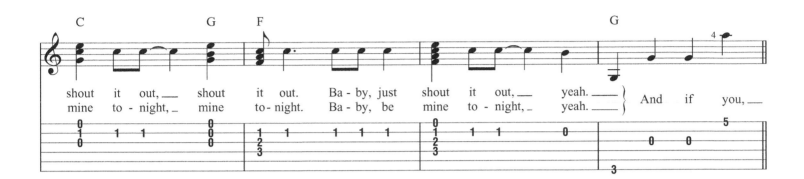

shout it out, _ shout it out. Ba - by, just shout it out, _ yeah. _____ } And if you, _
mine to-night, _ mine to-night. Ba - by, be mine to-night, _ yeah. _____

Pre-Chorus

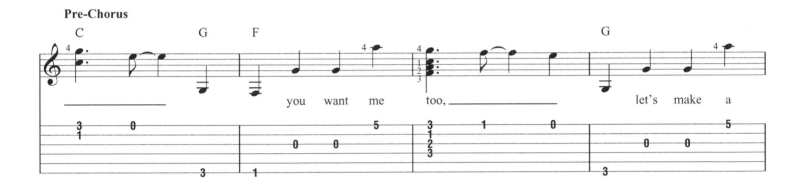

_____ you want me too, _____ let's make a

move. _____ Yeah! So tell me, girl, if ev-'ry time _ we _

Chorus
Half-time feel

tou - u - uch, you get this kind of ru - u - ush, ba - by, say,

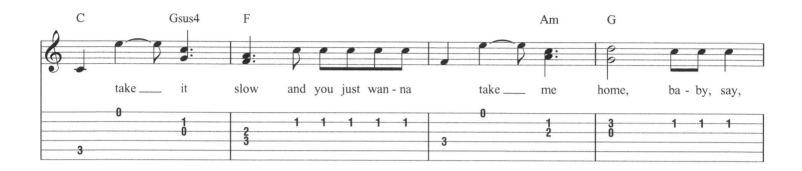

Bridge

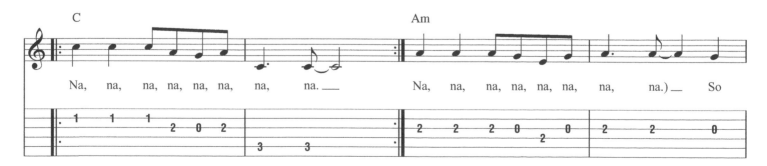

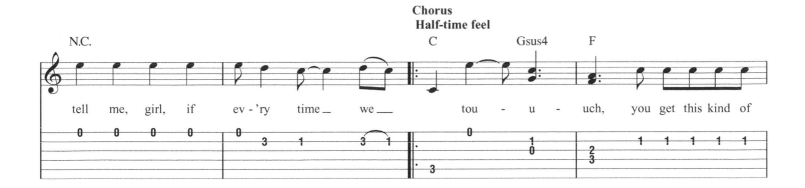

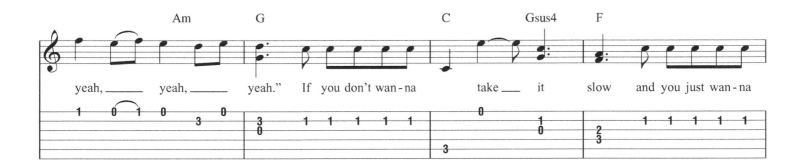

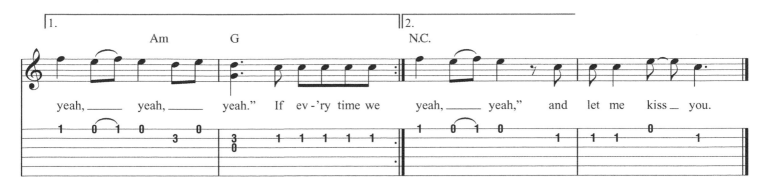

Little Things

Words and Music by Ed Sheeran and Fiona Bevan

Strum Pattern: 6
Pick Pattern: 2

1. Your hand fits in mine like it's made just for me, but bear this in mind: it was ___ meant to be. And I'm

3. You can't go to bed with- out a cup of tea, and may-be that's the rea-son that you talk ___ in your sleep. And

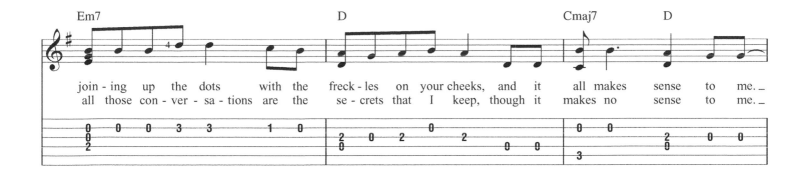

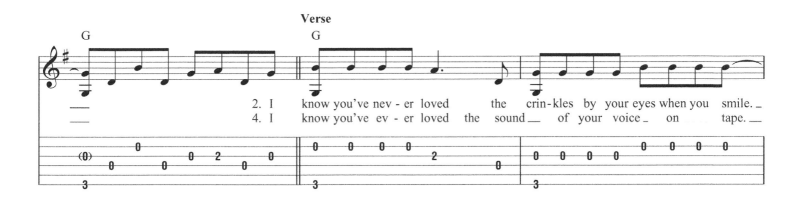

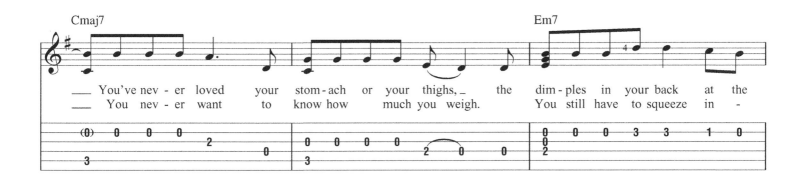

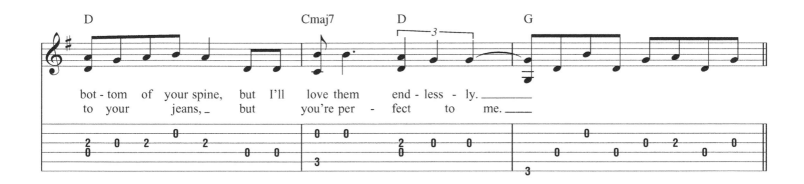

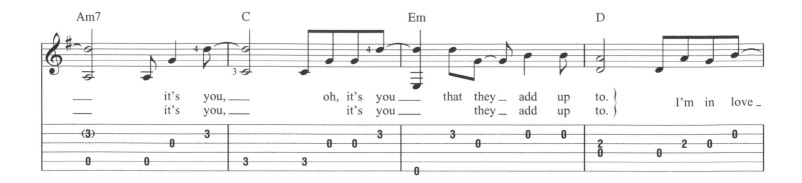

it's you, ___ oh, it's you ___ that they ___ add up to.
it's you, ___ it's you ___ they ___ add up to. } I'm in love ___

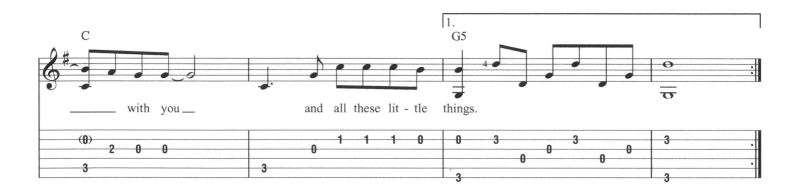

___ with you ___ and all these lit - tle things.

Bridge

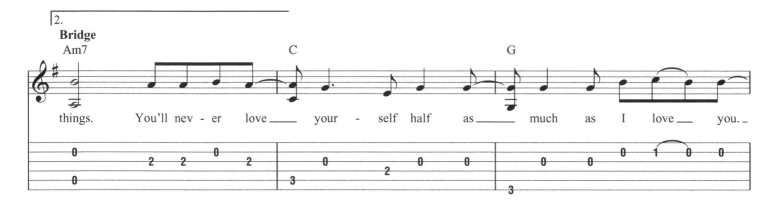

things. You'll nev - er love ___ your - self half as ___ much as I love ___ you. ___

And you'll nev - er treat ___ your - self right, dar -

ling, but I want you to. If I let you know ___

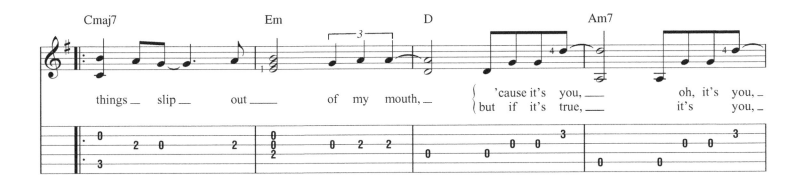

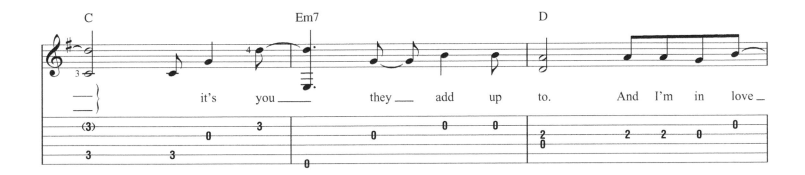

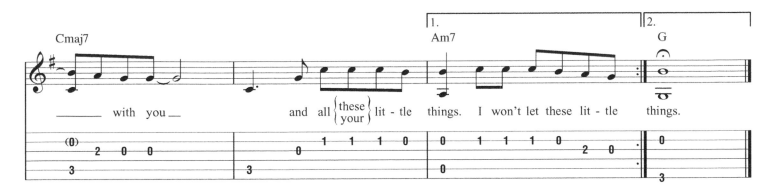

Live While We're Young

Words and Music by Rami Yacoub, Savan Kotecha and Carl Falk

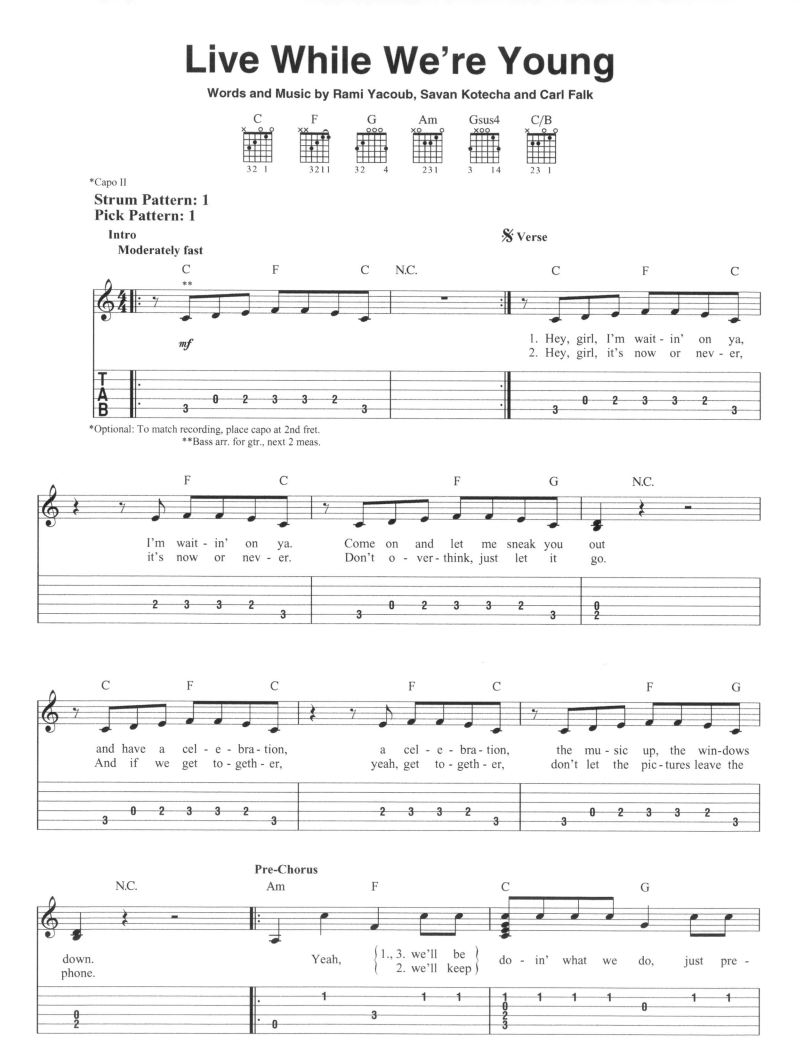

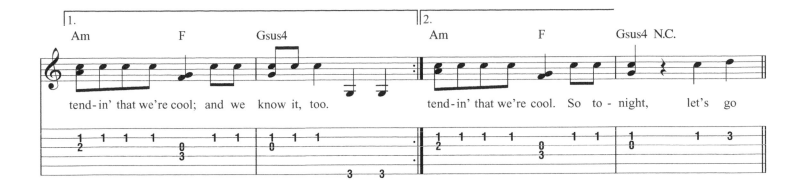

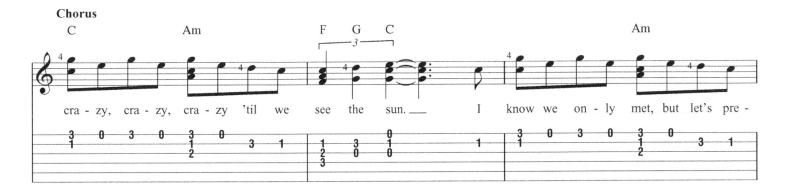

Chorus

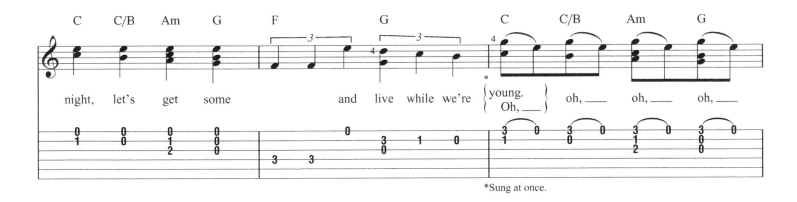

*Sung at once.

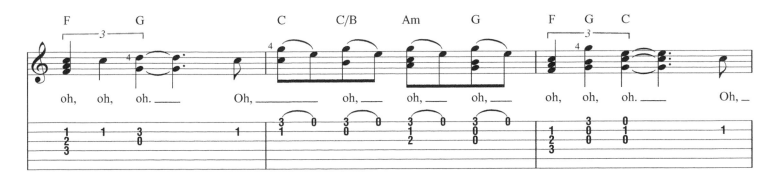

oh, ___ oh, ___ oh, ___ oh, oh, oh. ___ To - night, let's get some and live while we're

Interlude

D.S. al Coda
(take 2nd ending)

⊕ **Coda**
Bridge

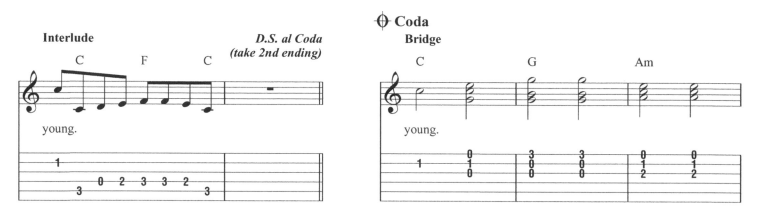

young.

young.

And girl, you and I, ___ we 'bout to make some

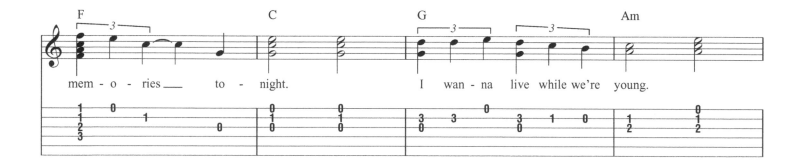

mem - o - ries ___ to - night. I wan - na live while we're young.

Chorus

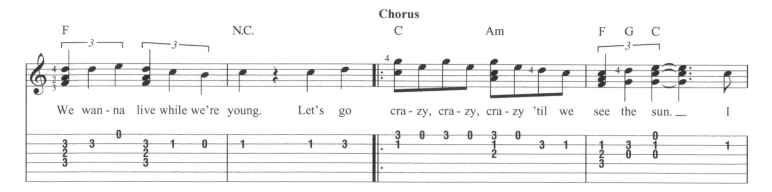

We wan - na live while we're young. Let's go cra - zy, cra - zy, cra - zy 'til we see the sun. ___ I

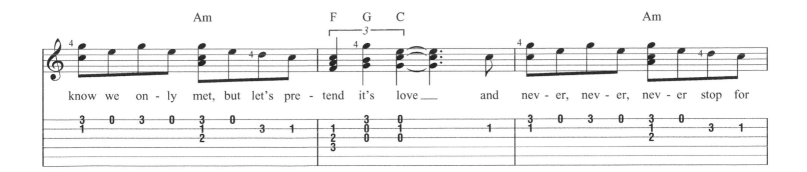

know we on-ly met, but let's pre-tend it's love ___ and nev-er, nev-er, nev-er stop for

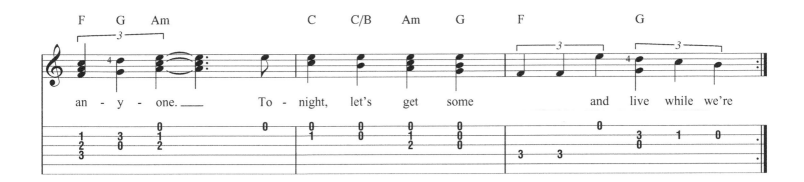

an-y-one. ___ To-night, let's get some and live while we're

Outro

young. Wan-na live, wan-na live, wan-na live while we're young. Wan-na live, wan-na

live, wan-na live while we're young. Wan-na live, wan-na live, wan-na live while... To-

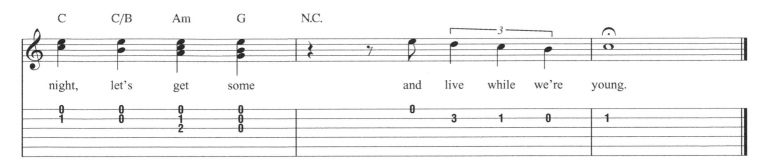

night, let's get some and live while we're young.

Midnight Memories

Words and Music by John Ryan, Jamie Scott, Julian Bunetta, Liam Payne and Louis Tomlinson

E5　E　A　D　A7　A6　C

C7　C6　D7　D6　B　C#m

Strum Pattern: 1
Pick Pattern: 1

Verse
Moderately slow, in 2

1. Straight off the plane to a new ho - tel. _____
2. Five foot some - thing with the skin - ny jeans. _____

Just touched down, you could
Don't look back, ba - by,

nev - er tell.
fol - low me.

Big house par - ty with a crowd - ed kitch - en.
don't know where I'm go - ing but I'm find - ing my way. _____

People talk, sh, but we don't lis - ten.
Same old sh, but a dif - f'rent day.

Pre-Chorus
Double-time feel

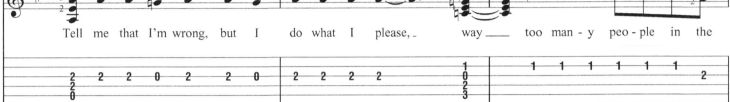

Tell me that I'm wrong, but I do what I please, _ way ___ too man - y peo - ple in the

Ad - di - son Lee. _ Now ___ I'm at the age when I know what I need, _ oh. _____

𝄋 **Chorus**
End double-time feel

Mid - night mem - o - ries. _

*3rd time, N.C., next 4 meas.

_ Oh, ___ oh, ___ oh. _____ Ba - by, you and me,

27

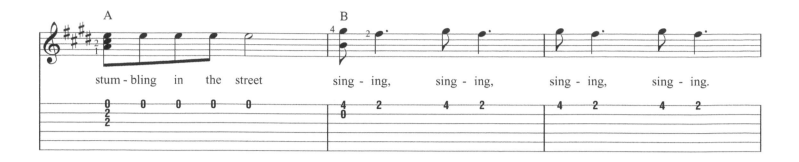

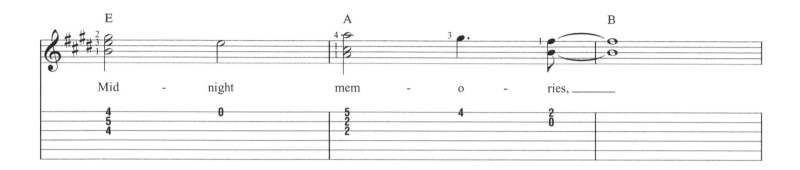

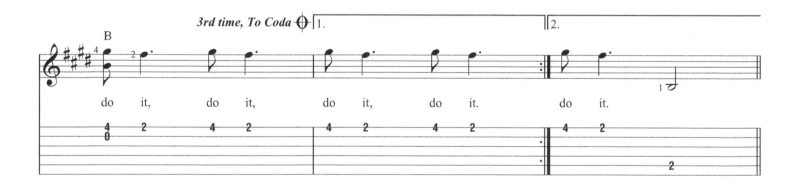

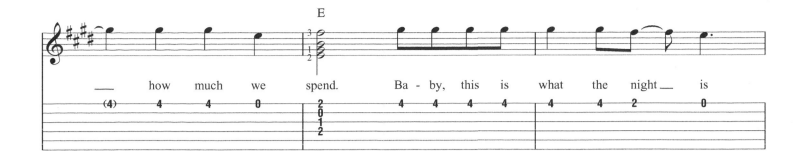

how much we spend. Ba - by, this is what the night ___ is

for. _____ I know noth -

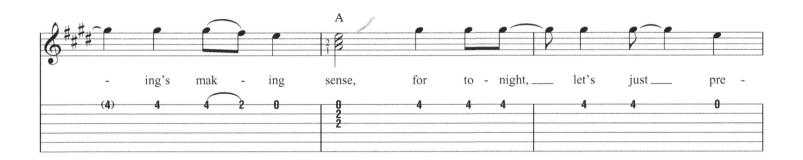

- ing's mak - ing sense, for to - night, ___ let's just ___ pre -

tend. I don't want to stop, so give ___ me more. _____

D.S. al Coda
End double-time feel

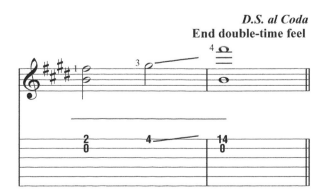

⊕ **Coda**

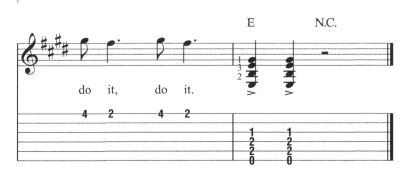

do it, do it.

One Thing

Words and Music by Savan Kotecha, Carl Falk and Rami Yacoub

*Capo II

Strum Pattern: 1
Pick Pattern: 1

*Optional: To match recording, place capo at 2nd fret.

Lyrics:

1. I've tried play-ing it cool, but when I'm look-ing at you, I can't ev-er be brave 'cause you make my heart race.

2. Shot me out of the

3. Now I'm climb-ing the

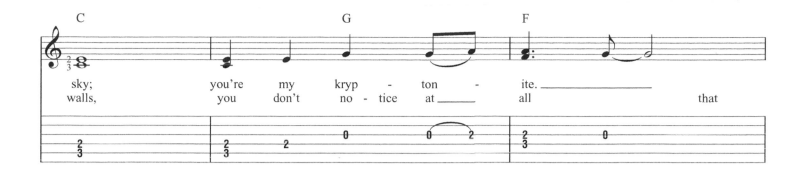

sky; you're my kryp - ton - ite. _____
walls, you don't no - tice at _____ all that

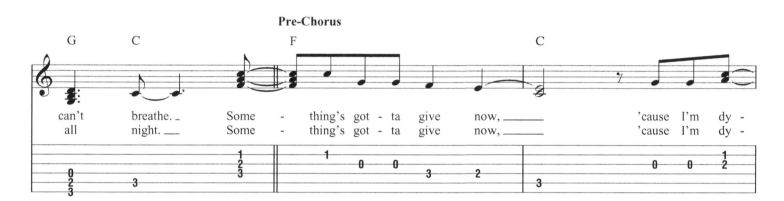

You keep mak - ing me weak; _____ yeah, fro - zen _____ and
I'm go - ing out of my mind _____ all day _____ and

Pre-Chorus

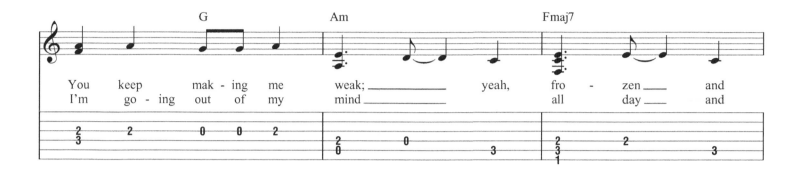

can't breathe. _ Some - thing's got - ta give now, _____ 'cause I'm dy-
all night. _ Some - thing's got - ta give now, _____ 'cause I'm dy -

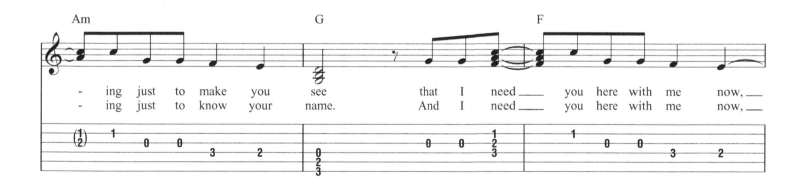

- ing just to make you see that I need _____ you here with me now, _____
- ing just to know your name. And I need _____ you here with me now, _____

'cause you've got _____ that one thing. So

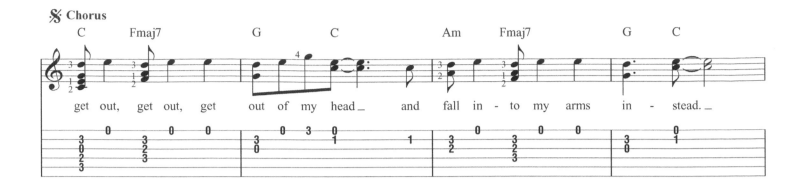

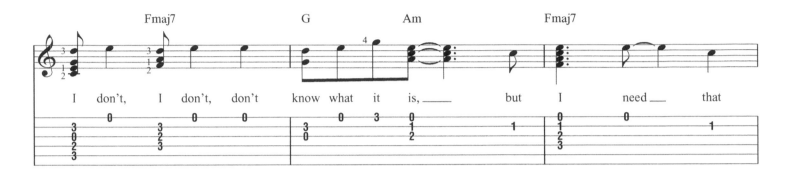

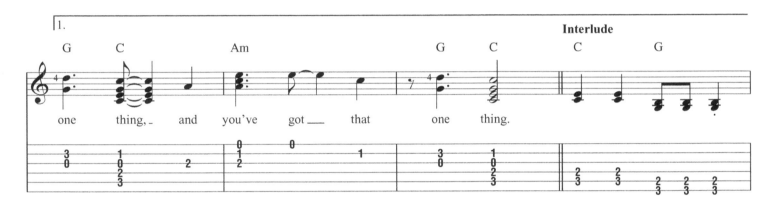

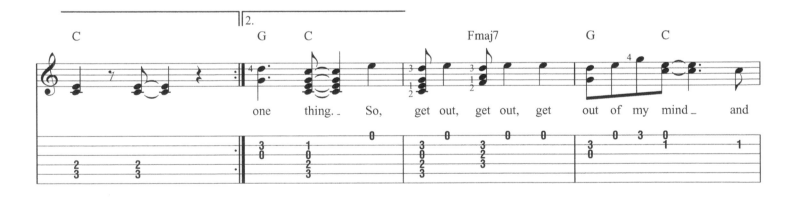

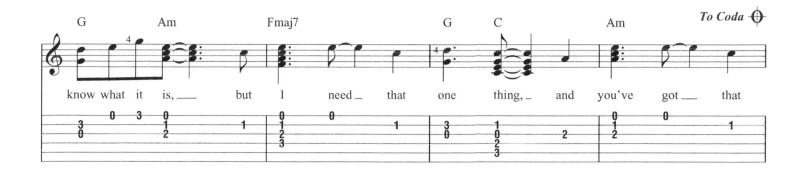

know what it is, ___ but I need ___ that one thing, ___ and you've got ___ that

Bridge

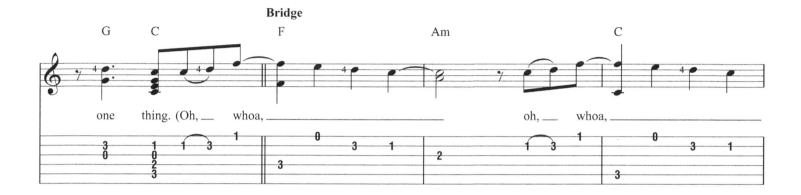

one thing. (Oh, ___ whoa, _____ oh, ___ whoa, _____

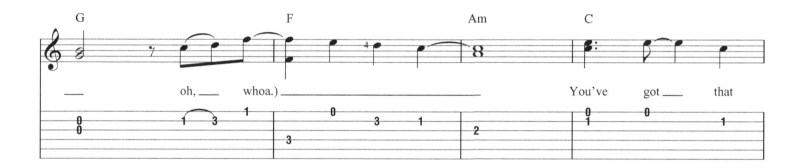

___ oh, ___ whoa.) _____ You've got ___ that

Chorus

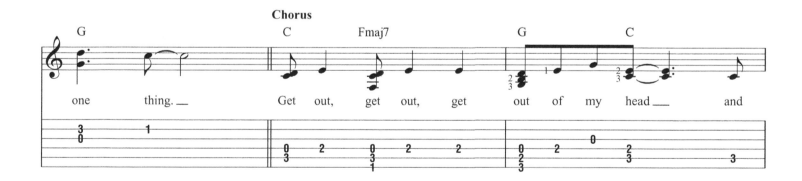

one thing. ___ Get out, get out, get out of my head ___ and

D.S. al Coda
(take 2nd ending) ✠ **Coda**

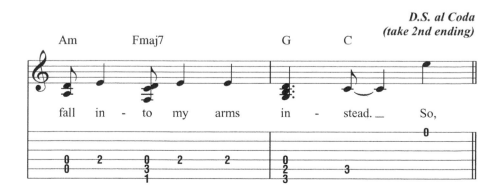

fall in - to my arms in - stead. ___ So,

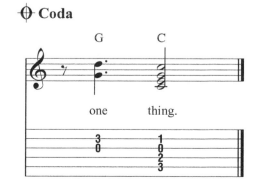

one thing.

Something Great

Words and Music by Gary Lightbody, Harry Styles and Jacknife Lee

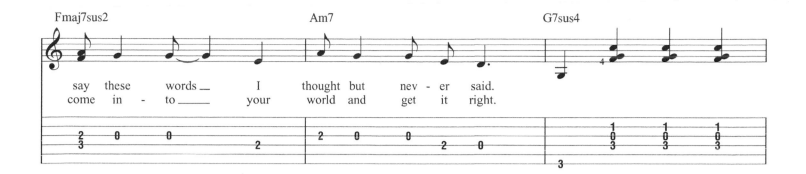

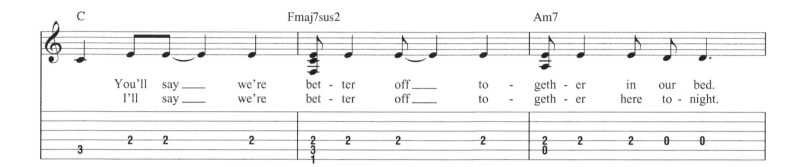

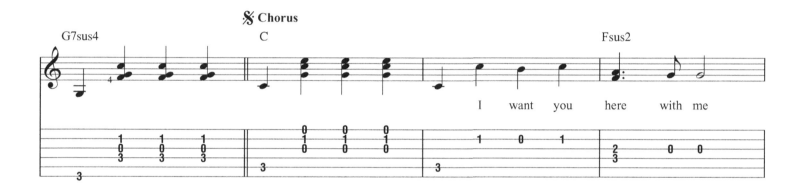

ev - 'ry - thing.   Is   it   too   much   to   ask   for   some - thing   great? __

Interlude

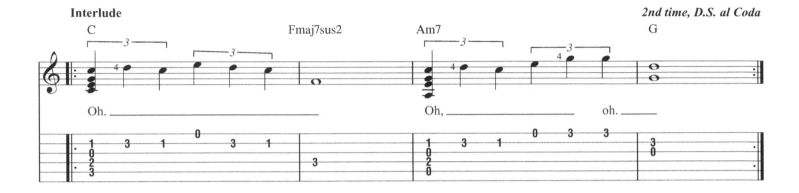

Oh. _____   Oh, _____   oh. _____

⊕ **Coda**

I   want   you   here   with   me   like   how   I

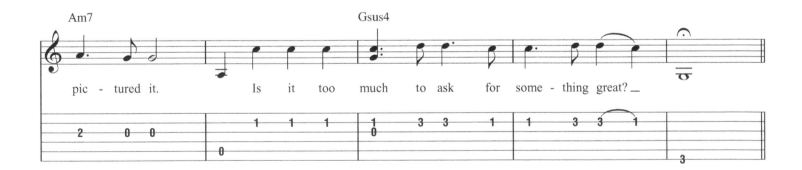

pic - tured it.   Is   it   too   much   to   ask   for   some - thing   great? __

Outro

You're   all __   I   want,   so   much__   it's   hurt - ing.

You & I

Words and Music by John Ryan, Jamie Scott and Julian Bunetta

right. Si - lence and sound,
night. Nev - er to - geth - er

did they ev - er hold each - oth - er
'cause they see things in a dif - f'rent

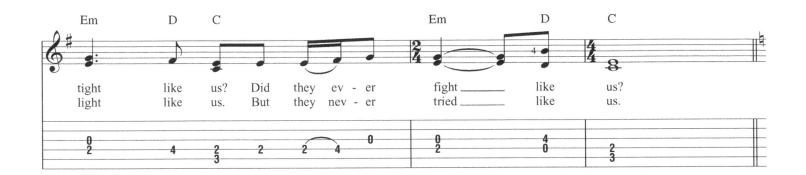

tight like us? Did they ev - er
light like us. But they nev - er

fight _____ like us?
tried _____ like us.

※ Chorus

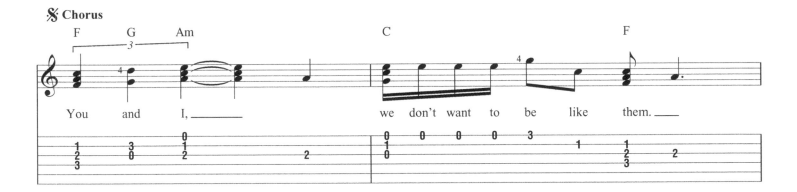

You and I, _____

we don't want to be like them. _____

We can make it 'til the end. _____

Noth - ing can come be - tween _____ you and I. _____

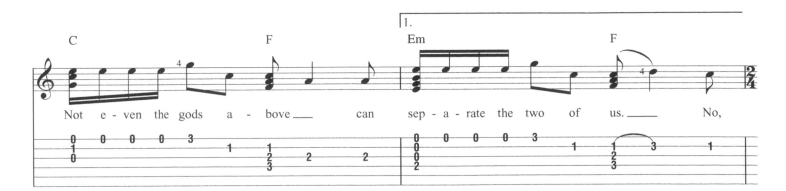

1.

Not e - ven the gods a - bove _____ can sep - a - rate the two of us. _____ No,

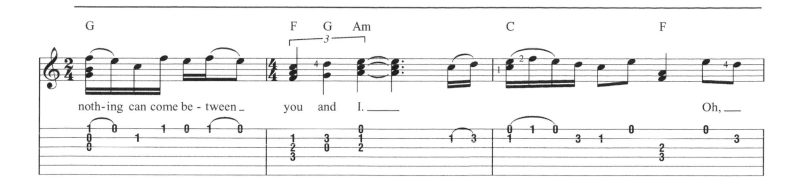

noth-ing can come be - tween __ you and I. __ Oh, __

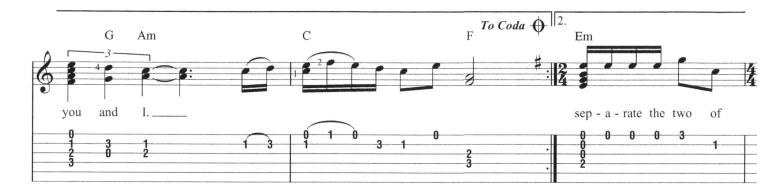

you and I. __ sep - a - rate the two of

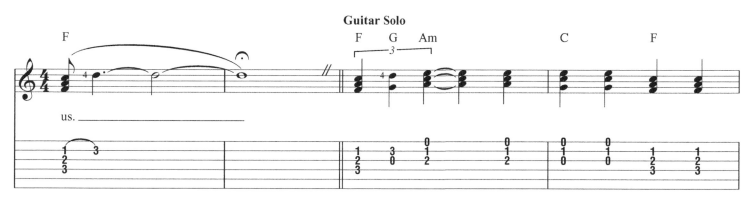

Guitar Solo

us. __

D.S. al Coda
(take 1st ending)

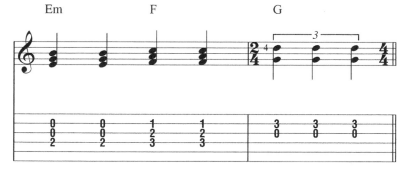

Coda
Outro

You and I. __

Repeat and fade

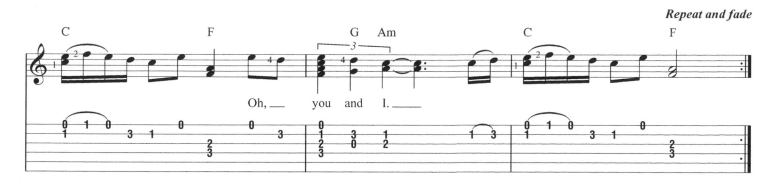

Oh, __ you and I.

Story of My Life

Words and Music by Jamie Scott, John Henry Ryan, Julian Bunetta,
Harry Styles, Liam Payne, Louis Tomlinson, Niall Horan and Zain Malik

*Capo III

Strum Pattern: 3
Pick Pattern: 3

*Optional: To match recording, place capo at 3rd fret.

1. Writ-ten in these walls are the sto-ries that I can't ex-
2. Writ-ten on these walls are the col-ors that I can't

plain.
change.
I leave my heart o-pen, but it stays right here emp-ty for
I leave my heart o-pen, but it stays right here ___ in its

days.
cage.
She told me in the morn-in' she don't feel the same a-bout us in her
I know that in the morn-in' now I see a sin-gle light up-on the

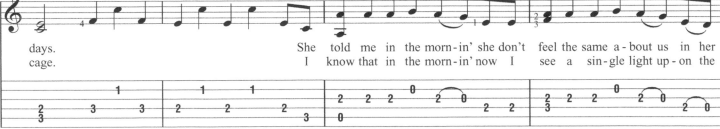

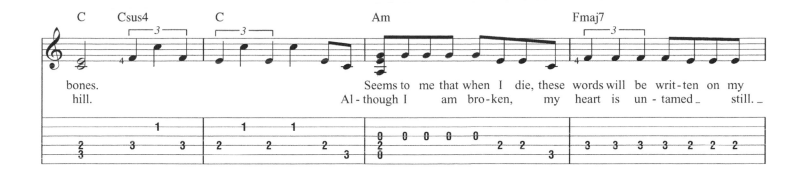

bones. / hill. Seems to me that when I die, these words will be writ-ten on my / Al-though I am bro-ken, my heart is un-tamed _ still. _

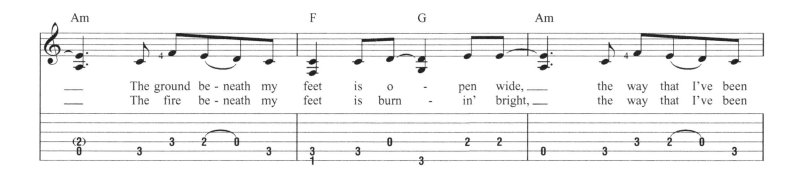

Pre-Chorus

stone. _____ And I'll be gone, gone to-night. _ / And I'll be gone, gone to-night. _

_ The ground be-neath my feet is o - pen wide, ___ the way that I've been / _ The fire be-neath my feet is burn - in' bright, ___ the way that I've been

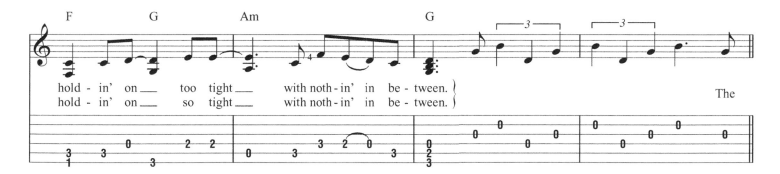

hold - in' on ___ too tight ___ with noth-in' in be - tween. } / hold - in' on ___ so tight ___ with noth-in' in be - tween. } The

Chorus

sto - ry of my life. I take her home. _ I drive all night _ to keep her warm _____ and

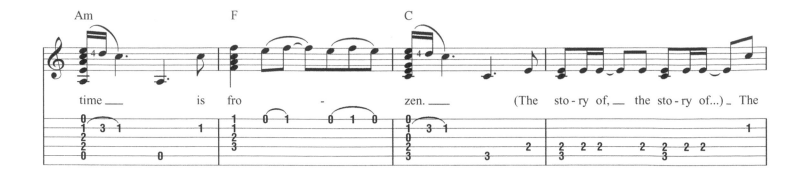

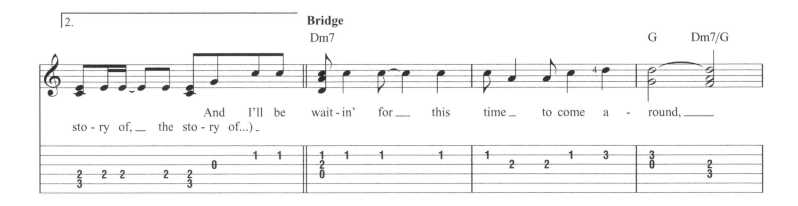

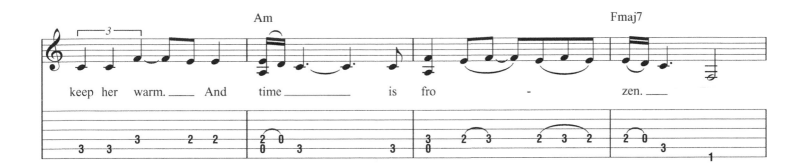

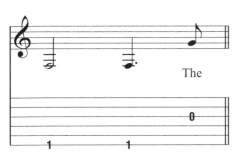

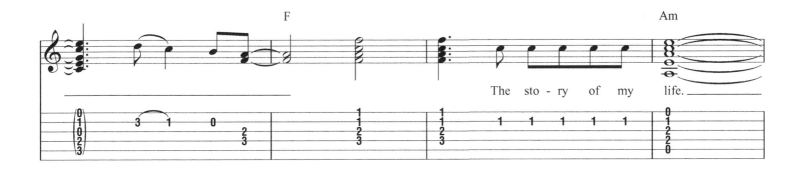

Strong

Words and Music by John Ryan, Jamie Scott, Julian Bunetta and Louis Tomlinson

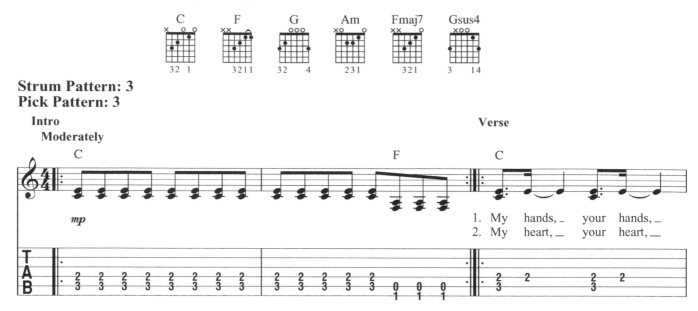

Strum Pattern: 3
Pick Pattern: 3

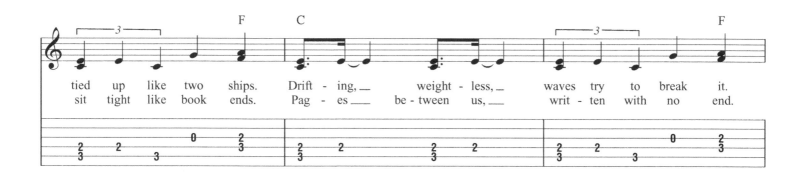

1. My hands,__ your hands,__
2. My heart,__ your heart,__

tied up like two ships. Drift - ing,__ weight - less,__ waves try to break it.
sit tight like book ends. Pag - es__ be - tween us,__ writ - ten with no end.

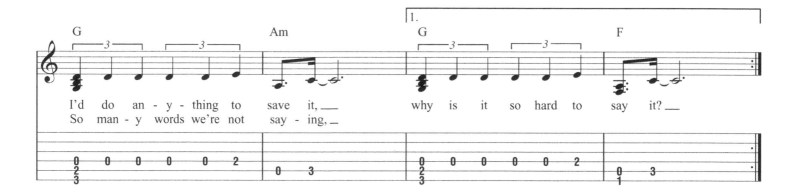

I'd do an - y - thing to save it,__ why is it so hard to say it?__
So man - y words we're not say - ing,__

don't want to wait 'til it's gone, you make me strong. I'm

sor - ry if I say, "I need you." — But I don't care, I'm not scared of

love. _____ 'Cause when I'm not with you, I'm weak - er. Is that so wrong, is it so

wrong that you make me strong?

Verse

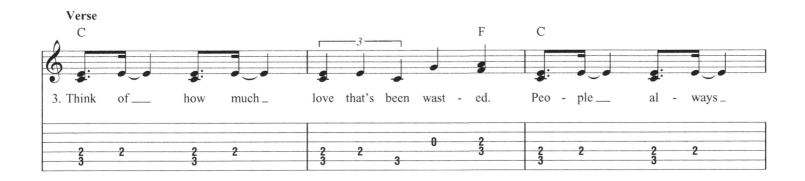

3. Think of ___ how much ___ love that's been wast - ed. Peo - ple ___ al - ways ___

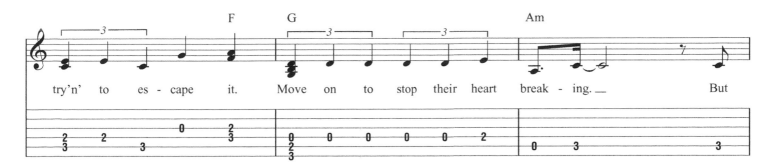

try'n' to es - cape it. Move on to stop their heart break - ing. ___ But

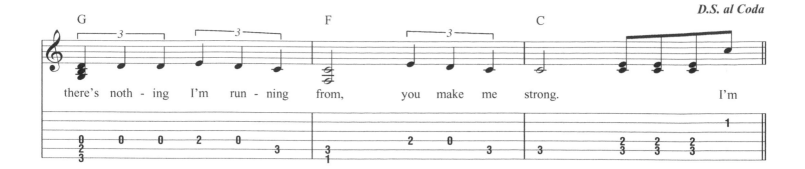

there's noth - ing I'm run - ning from, you make me strong. I'm

Coda

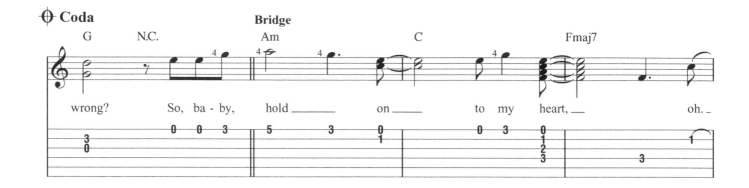

wrong? So, ba - by, hold _____ on _____ to my heart, _____ oh. _____

_____ Need you to keep me from fall - ing a - part. _____

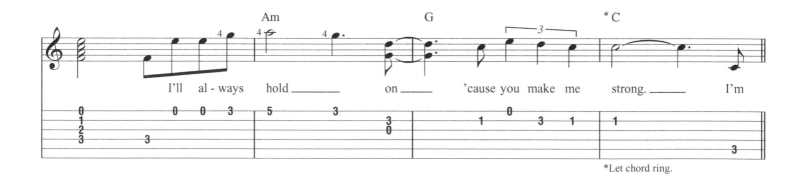

I'll al - ways hold _____ on _____ 'cause you make me strong. _____ I'm

*Let chord ring.

Chorus

sor - ry if I say, "I need you." _ But I don't care, I'm not scared of

love. _____ 'Cause when I'm not with you, I'm weak-er. Is that so

wrong, is it so wrong? I'm sor-ry if I say, "I need you." __ But I

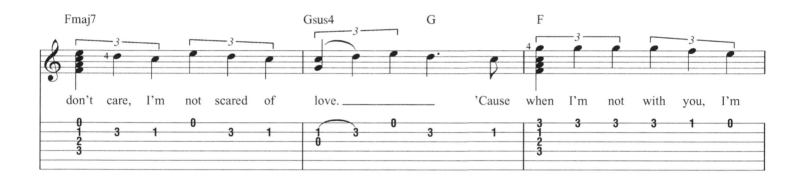

don't care, I'm not scared of love. _____ 'Cause when I'm not with you, I'm

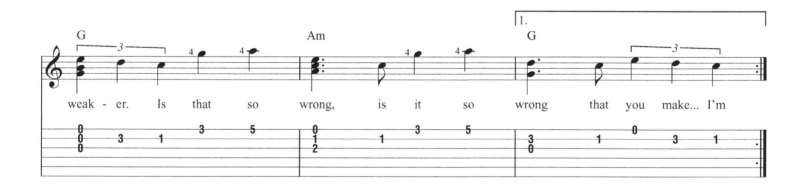

weak-er. Is that so wrong, is it so wrong that you make... I'm

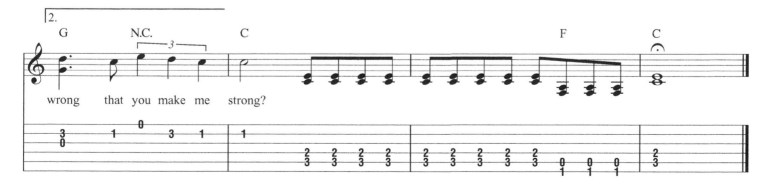

wrong that you make me strong?

Up All Night

Words and Music by Savan Kotecha and Matt Squire

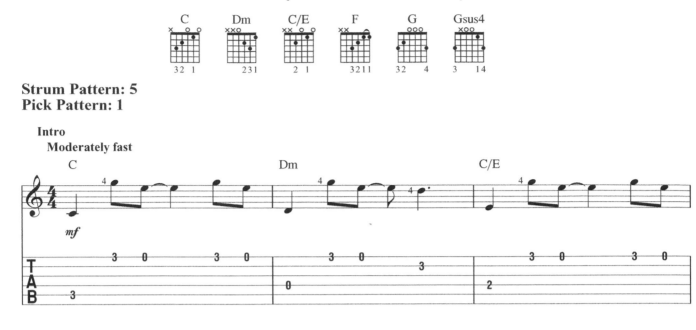

Strum Pattern: 5
Pick Pattern: 1

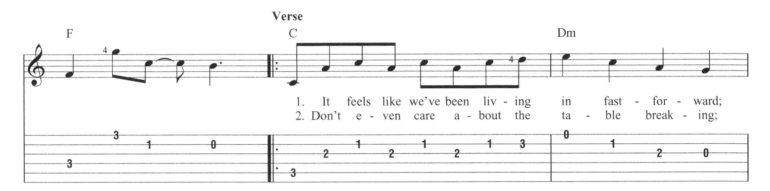

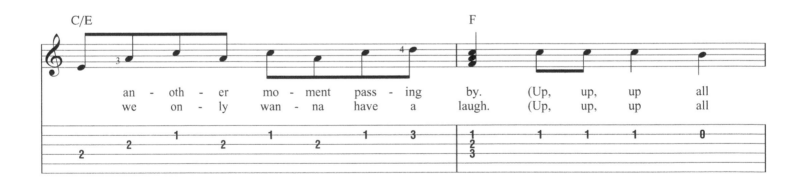

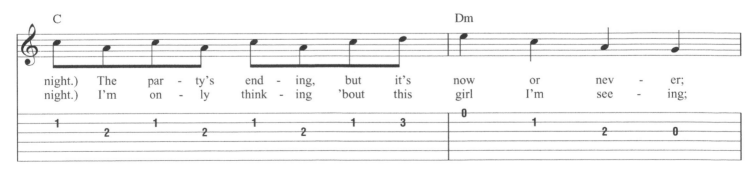

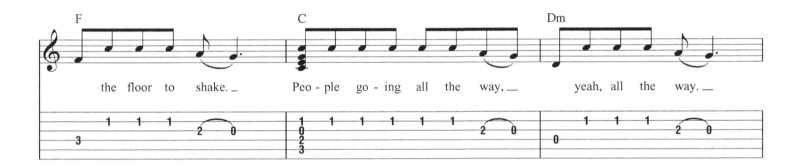

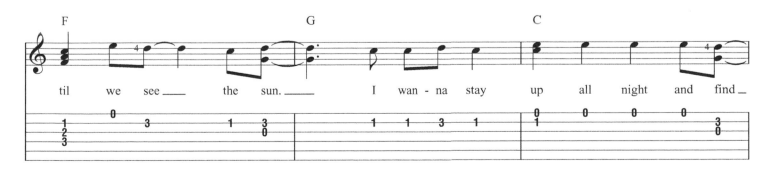

— a girl — and tell her she's — the one. — Hold on to the

feel - ing and don't let it go, 'cause we got the floor now. Get out of con -

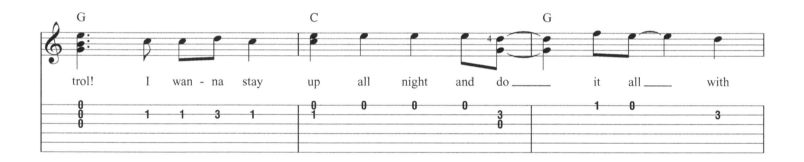

trol! I wan - na stay up all night and do — it all — with

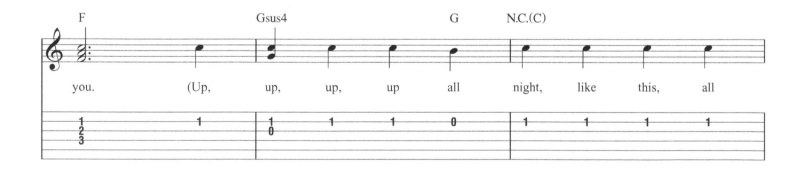

you. (Up, up, up, up all night, like this, all

3rd time, To Coda ⊕

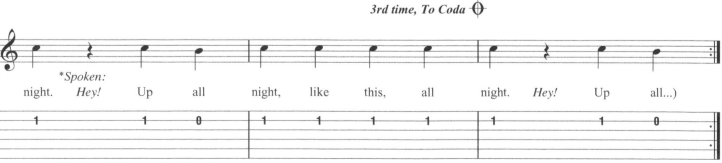

*Spoken:
night. *Hey!* Up all night, like this, all night. *Hey!* Up all...)

*Lyrics in italics are spoken throughout.

Bridge

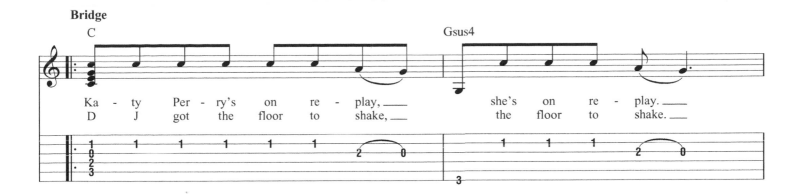

Ka - ty Per - ry's on re - play, ___ she's on re - play. ___
D J got the floor to shake, ___ the floor to shake. ___

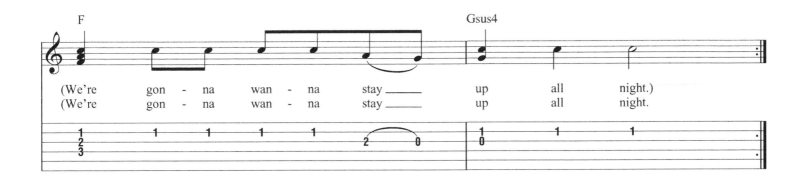

(We're gon - na wan - na stay ___ up all night.)
(We're gon - na wan - na stay ___ up all night.

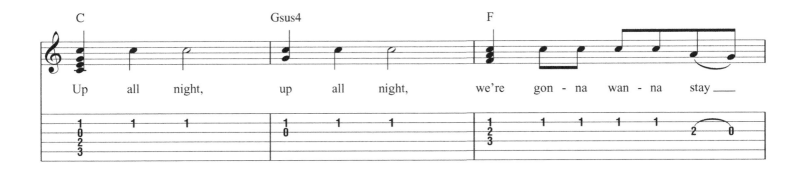

Up all night, up all night, we're gon - na wan - na stay ___

D.S. al Coda

up all...) Ah, ___ ee, ah. ___ I wan - na stay

Coda

night. *Hey!* Up all night.)

What Makes You Beautiful

Words and Music by Savan Kotecha, Rami Yacoub and Carl Falk

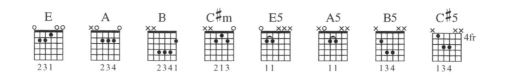

Strum Pattern: 3
Pick Pattern: 3

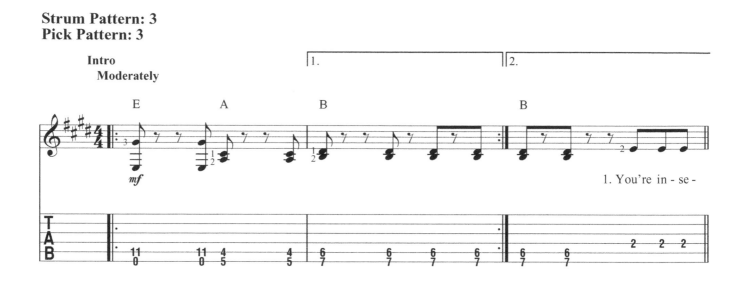

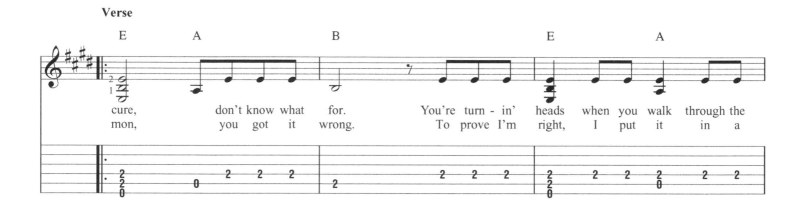

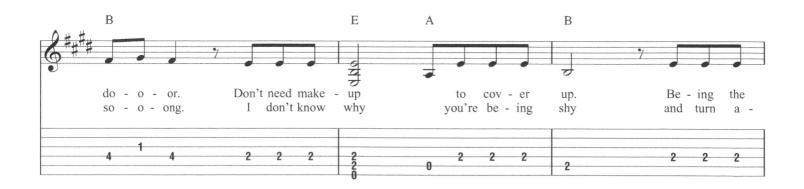

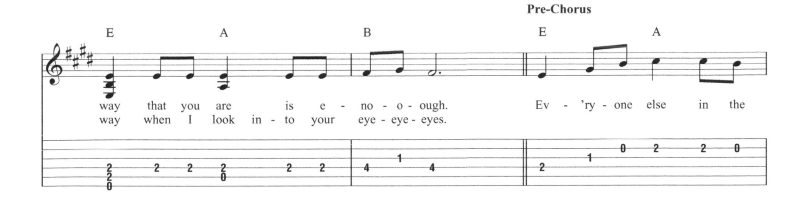

way that you are is e - no - o - ough.
way when I look in - to your eye - eye - eyes.

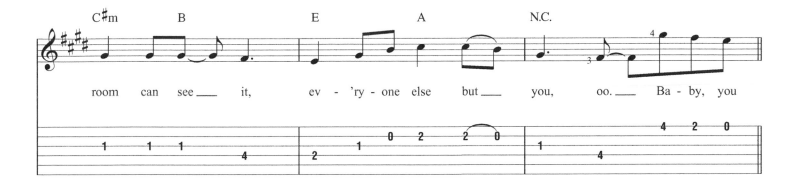

room can see — it, ev - 'ry - one else but — you, oo. — Ba - by, you

%Chorus

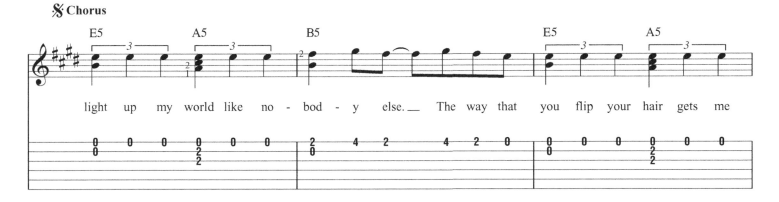

light up my world like no - bod - y else. — The way that you flip your hair gets me

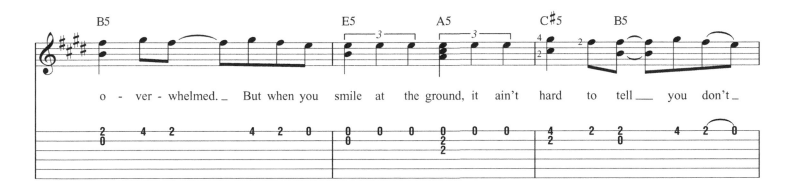

o - ver - whelmed. — But when you smile at the ground, it ain't hard to tell — you don't —

know - oh - oh, you don't know you're beau - ti - ful. If on - ly you saw what

*Chords in parentheses played 3rd time.

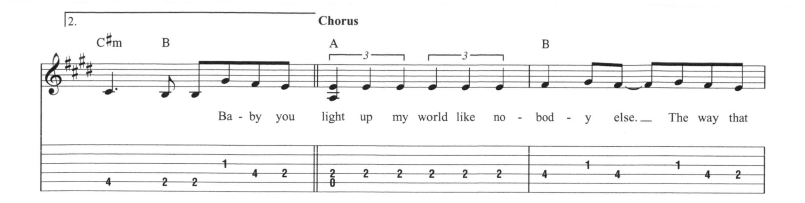

Ba-by you light up my world like no-bod-y else.__ The way that

you flip your hair gets me o-ver-whelmed.__ But when you smile at the ground, it ain't

D.S. al Coda

hard to tell__ you don't__ know - oh - oh, you don't know you're beau - ti - ful. / Ba - by, you

*Sung at once.

⊕ Coda

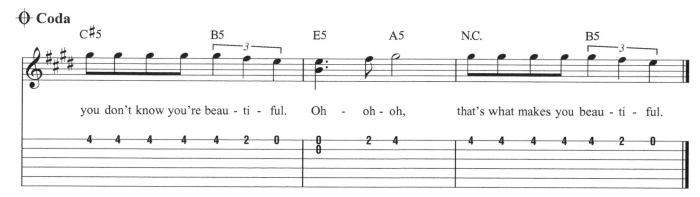

you don't know you're beau - ti - ful. Oh - oh - oh, that's what makes you beau - ti - ful.

EASY GUITAR WITH NOTES & TAB

This series features simplified arrangements with notes, tab, chord charts, and strum and pick patterns.

MIXED FOLIOS

00702287	Acoustic	$19.99
00702002	Acoustic Rock Hits for Easy Guitar	$15.99
00702166	All-Time Best Guitar Collection	$19.99
00702232	Best Acoustic Songs for Easy Guitar	$16.99
00119835	Best Children's Songs	$16.99
00703055	The Big Book of Nursery Rhymes & Children's Songs	$16.99
00698978	Big Christmas Collection	$19.99
00702394	Bluegrass Songs for Easy Guitar	$15.99
00289632	Bohemian Rhapsody	$19.99
00703387	Celtic Classics	$14.99
00224808	Chart Hits of 2016-2017	$14.99
00267383	Chart Hits of 2017-2018	$14.99
00334293	Chart Hits of 2019-2020	$16.99
00702149	Children's Christian Songbook	$9.99
00702028	Christmas Classics	$8.99
00101779	Christmas Guitar	$14.99
00702141	Classic Rock	$8.95
00159642	Classical Melodies	$12.99
00253933	Disney/Pixar's Coco	$16.99
00702203	CMT's 100 Greatest Country Songs	$34.99
00702283	The Contemporary Christian Collection	$16.99
00196954	Contemporary Disney	$19.99
00702239	Country Classics for Easy Guitar	$24.99

00702257	Easy Acoustic Guitar Songs	$16.99
00702041	Favorite Hymns for Easy Guitar	$12.99
00222701	Folk Pop Songs	$17.99
00126894	Frozen	$14.99
00333922	Frozen 2	$14.99
00702286	Glee	$16.99
00702160	The Great American Country Songbook	$19.99
00702148	Great American Gospel for Guitar	$14.99
00702050	Great Classical Themes for Easy Guitar	$9.99
00275088	The Greatest Showman	$17.99
00148030	Halloween Guitar Songs	$14.99
00702273	Irish Songs	$12.99
00192503	Jazz Classics for Easy Guitar	$16.99
00702275	Jazz Favorites for Easy Guitar	$17.99
00702274	Jazz Standards for Easy Guitar	$19.99
00702162	Jumbo Easy Guitar Songbook	$24.99
00232285	La La Land	$16.99
00702258	Legends of Rock	$14.99
00702189	MTV's 100 Greatest Pop Songs	$34.99
00702272	1950s Rock	$16.99
00702271	1960s Rock	$16.99
00702270	1970s Rock	$19.99
00702269	1980s Rock	$15.99
00702268	1990s Rock	$19.99
00369043	Rock Songs for Kids	$14.99

00109725	Once	$14.99
00702187	Selections from O Brother Where Art Thou?	$19.99
00702178	100 Songs for Kids	$14.99
00702515	Pirates of the Caribbean	$17.99
00702125	Praise and Worship for Guitar	$14.99
00287930	Songs from *A Star Is Born, The Greatest Showman, La La Land*, and More Movie Musicals	$16.99
00702285	Southern Rock Hits	$12.99
00156420	Star Wars Music	$16.99
00121535	30 Easy Celtic Guitar Solos	$16.99
00702156	3-Chord Rock	$12.99
00244654	Top Hits of 2017	$14.99
00283786	Top Hits of 2018	$14.99
00702294	Top Worship Hits	$17.99
00702255	VH1's 100 Greatest Hard Rock Songs	$34.99
00702175	VH1's 100 Greatest Songs of Rock and Roll	$29.99
00702253	Wicked	$12.99

ARTIST COLLECTIONS

00702267	AC/DC for Easy Guitar	$16.99
00702598	Adele for Easy Guitar	$15.99
00156221	Adele – 25	$16.99
00702040	Best of the Allman Brothers	$16.99
00702865	J.S. Bach for Easy Guitar	$15.99
00702169	Best of The Beach Boys	$15.99
00702292	The Beatles — 1	$22.99
00125796	Best of Chuck Berry	$15.99
00702201	The Essential Black Sabbath	$15.99
00702250	blink-182 — Greatest Hits	$17.99
02501615	Zac Brown Band — The Foundation	$17.99
02501621	Zac Brown Band — You Get What You Give	$16.99
00702043	Best of Johnny Cash	$17.99
00702090	Eric Clapton's Best	$16.99
00702086	Eric Clapton — from the Album Unplugged	$17.99
00702202	The Essential Eric Clapton	$17.99
00702053	Best of Patsy Cline	$15.99
00222697	Very Best of Coldplay – 2nd Edition	$16.99
00702229	The Very Best of Creedence Clearwater Revival	$16.99
00702145	Best of Jim Croce	$16.99
00702278	Crosby, Stills & Nash	$12.99
14042809	Bob Dylan	$15.99
00702276	Fleetwood Mac — Easy Guitar Collection	$17.99
00139462	The Very Best of Grateful Dead	$16.99
00702136	Best of Merle Haggard	$16.99
00702227	Jimi Hendrix — Smash Hits	$19.99
00702288	Best of Hillsong United	$12.99
00702236	Best of Antonio Carlos Jobim	$15.99
00702245	Elton John — Greatest Hits 1970–2002	$19.99

00129855	Jack Johnson	$16.99
00702204	Robert Johnson	$14.99
00702234	Selections from Toby Keith — 35 Biggest Hits	$12.95
00702003	Kiss	$16.99
00702216	Lynyrd Skynyrd	$16.99
00702182	The Essential Bob Marley	$16.99
00146081	Maroon 5	$14.99
00121925	Bruno Mars – Unorthodox Jukebox	$12.99
00702248	Paul McCartney — All the Best	$14.99
00125484	The Best of MercyMe	$12.99
00702209	Steve Miller Band — Young Hearts (Greatest Hits)	$12.95
00124167	Jason Mraz	$15.99
00702096	Best of Nirvana	$16.99
00702211	The Offspring — Greatest Hits	$17.99
00138026	One Direction	$17.99
00702030	Best of Roy Orbison	$17.99
00702144	Best of Ozzy Osbourne	$14.99
00702279	Tom Petty	$17.99
00102911	Pink Floyd	$17.99
00702139	Elvis Country Favorites	$19.99
00702293	The Very Best of Prince	$19.99
00699415	Best of Queen for Guitar	$16.99
00109279	Best of R.E.M.	$14.99
00702208	Red Hot Chili Peppers — Greatest Hits	$16.99
00198960	The Rolling Stones	$17.99
00174793	The Very Best of Santana	$16.99
00702196	Best of Bob Seger	$16.99
00146046	Ed Sheeran	$15.99
00702252	Frank Sinatra — Nothing But the Best	$12.99
00702010	Best of Rod Stewart	$17.99
00702049	Best of George Strait	$17.99

00702259	Taylor Swift for Easy Guitar	$15.99
00359800	Taylor Swift – Easy Guitar Anthology	$24.99
00702260	Taylor Swift — Fearless	$14.99
00139727	Taylor Swift — 1989	$17.99
00115960	Taylor Swift — Red	$16.99
00253667	Taylor Swift — Reputation	$17.99
00702290	Taylor Swift — Speak Now	$16.99
00232849	Chris Tomlin Collection – 2nd Edition	$14.99
00702226	Chris Tomlin — See the Morning	$12.95
00148643	Train	$14.99
00702427	U2 — 18 Singles	$19.99
00702108	Best of Stevie Ray Vaughan	$17.99
00279005	The Who	$14.99
00702123	Best of Hank Williams	$15.99
00194548	Best of John Williams	$14.99
00702228	Neil Young — Greatest Hits	$17.99
00119133	Neil Young — Harvest	$14.99

Prices, contents and availability subject to change without notice.

Visit Hal Leonard online at **halleonard.com**